D0408213

How to Survive
in Suburbia
When Your Heart's
in the Himalayas

How to Survive in Suburbia When Your Heart's in the Himalayas

by Gwen Davis

Wyden Books

FIRST EDITION

Text design by Bob Antler

Photographs by Bob Antler, Jerry Kresch and Bob Hunsicker.

Photo on pages 184-85 courtesy of The Museum of Modern Art/Film Stills Archive.

Library of Congress Cataloging in Publication Data
Davis, Gwen.
   How to survive in suburbia when your heart's in the Himalayas.

   I. Title.
PS3554.A9346H6   170'.202   76-46277
ISBN 0-671-22404-2

For
Diane Brown,
Rhea Kohan,
Muggy Hoffman,
Rosemarie Stack,
Sally Nevius
and all of us.

How to Survive
in Suburbia
When Your Heart's
in the Himalayas

Think of carpool as Karma.

Give imaginary interviews to Time magazin

while peeling potatoes.   Stress your best qualities.

A bird's singing doesn't mean it isn't depressed.

Your ship cannot come in until yo

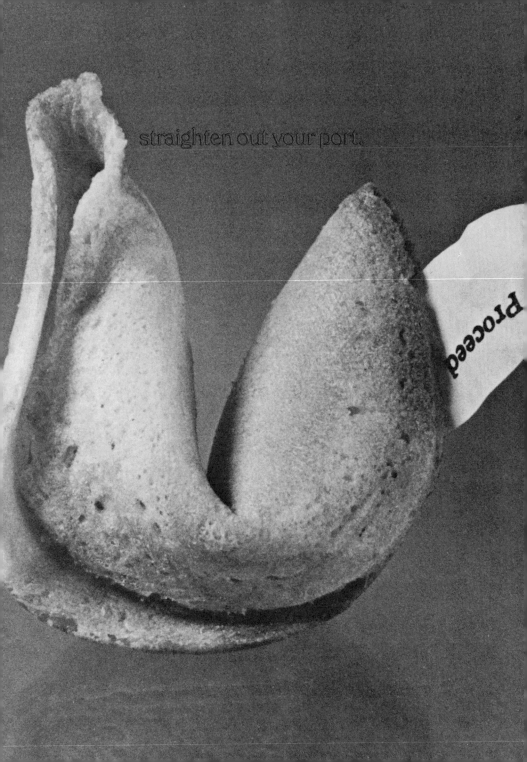
straighten out your port.

Proceed

Do not join Encounter groups.
If you enjoy being made to feel inadequate,
call your Mother.

Everyone you know can tell you how
terrible things are. Be original.
Learn to see the bright side.

To get a bee to go away, close your eyes
and think loving thoughts about everyone
you know, especially those who would enjoy
your being stung by a bee.

Pain is to courage what flour is to pancakes.

Jane Fonda isn't as cute as she used to be, either.

Have a mental garage sale. Get rid of all t

oughts you don't really need.

Remember how much you wanted to get married.

See crabgrass as

an assertion of spirit on the part of weeds.

You are spirit, crystallized in time.
Tell that to your dishwasher.

Do not confuse courage
with being pushy,
except at the P.T.A.

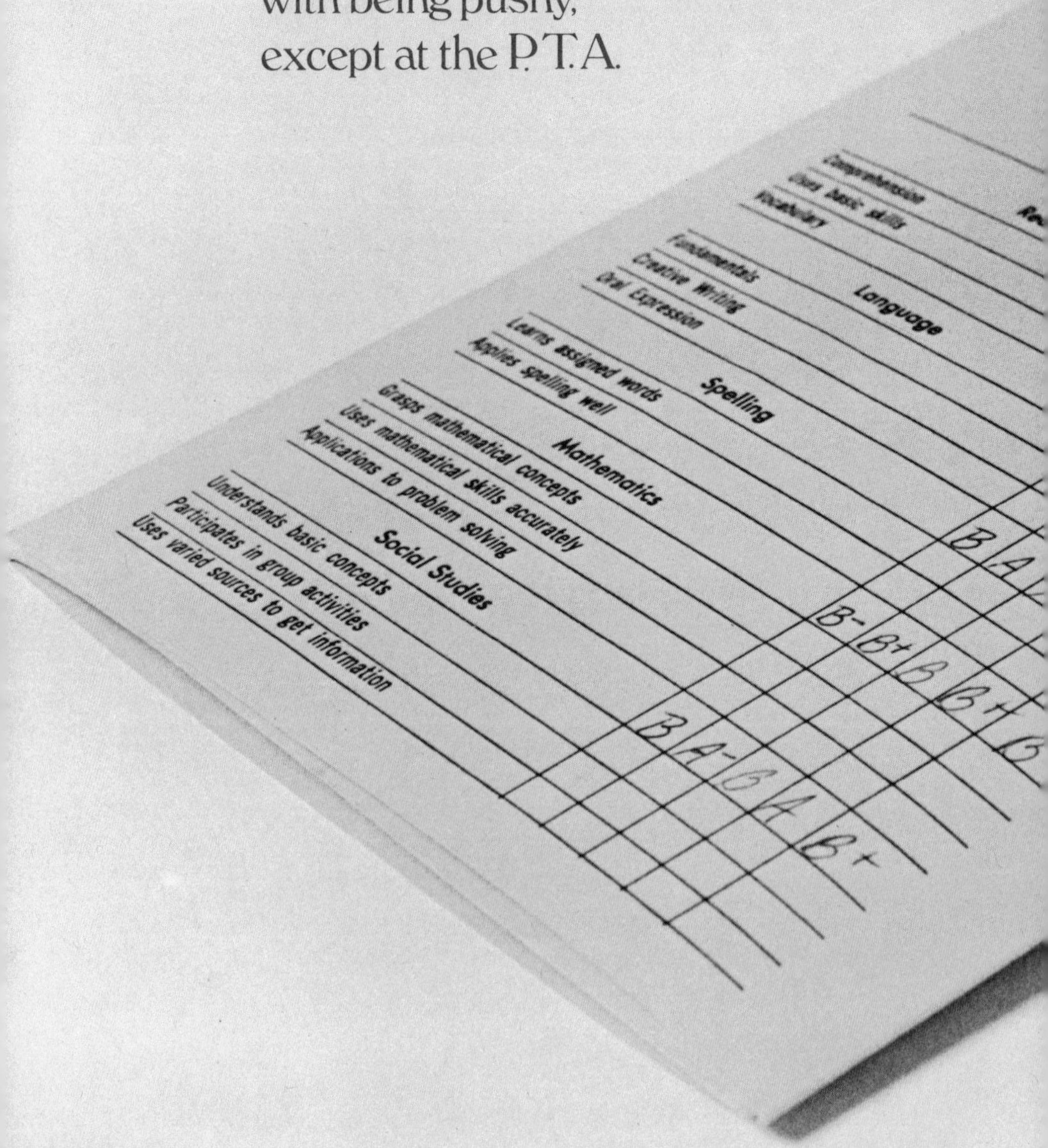

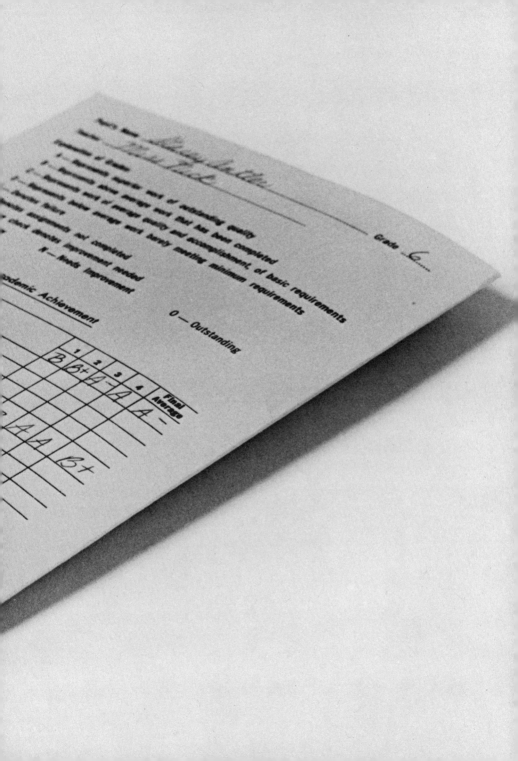

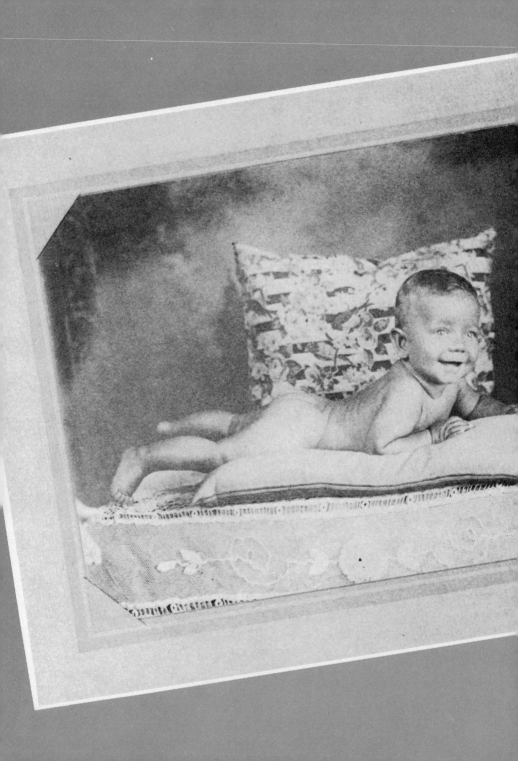

If you are sad that your children
won't stay babies, get a dog.

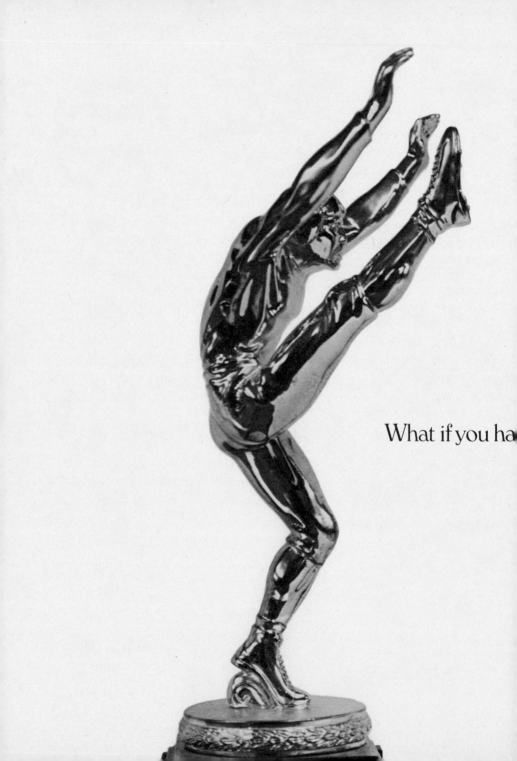

What if you ha

tten the boy you loved in high school?

Nothing worth having was ever gotten easily.

ncluding the special at Safeway.

If God meant us to eat meat,
He wouldn't have made it
so expensive.

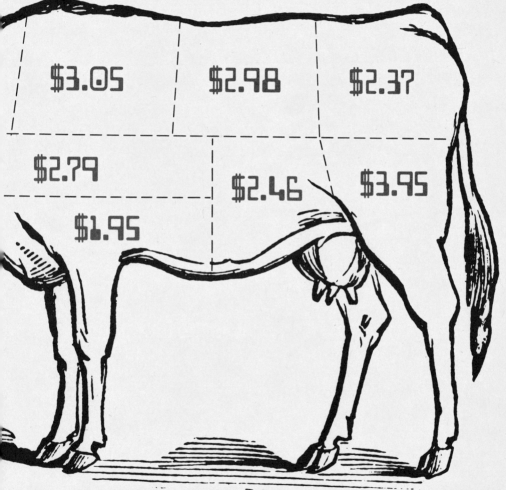

Today is the first day of the rest

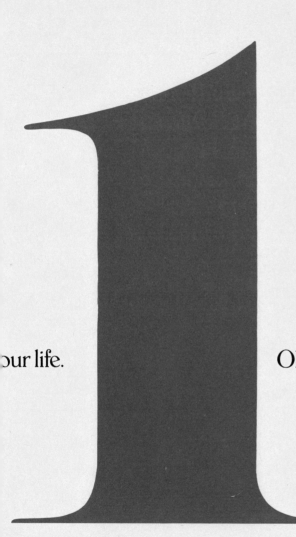

our life.   Oh my God.

Man's reach should exceed his grasp

r what is yoga for?

Appreciate a sunset

Maybe even God has a need for approval.

Nicotine dulls your sexual feelings.
That ought to help you quit.

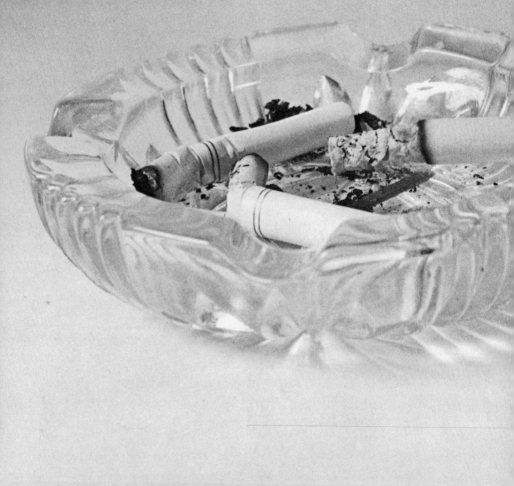

Did you ever dream when you were a Girl Scou

at leaders manipulated?

Make your life an open book,
but only if the movies will buy it.

Am I my house's keeper?

Women, like wine, are tastier for a little aging.
Help spread the rumor.

Curiosity may have killed the cat,
but it was better than
being bored to death.

Even a fading rose has beauty to it
if you set it in the right light.

Put it in a softly sunny place and study it.
Then do the same with yourself.

If you can't manage that,

have a quick nervous breakdown.

Collect treasures that have meaning only to you. Put them in a special place, and explain them to no one, except when you're giving interviews to <u>Time</u> magazine.

Cultivate night-blooming jasmine near your bedroom window, and dream of men you've always longed for.

Or, cultivate men you've always longed f

...nd go back to sleep.

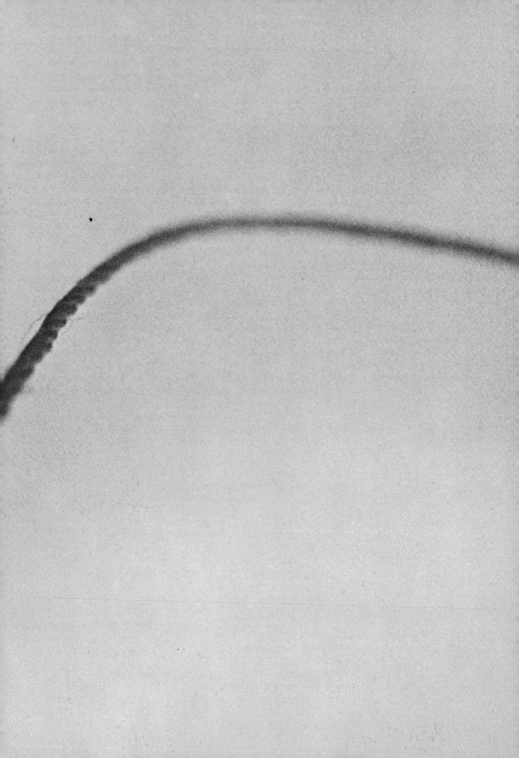

Try not to envy those who are naturally neat.

Remember that reality is an illusion, too.

Hope is on the other side of despair.
Get to despair, pass through it,
and leave it behind you.

MUNICIPAL COURT, BOROUGH OF PRINCETON
MONUMENT DRIVE, COUNTY OF MERCER
SUMMONS — YOU ARE HEREBY SUMMONED TO APPEAR PERSON-
ALLY BEFORE THIS COURT TO ANSWER THE FOLLOWING OFFENSE:

C 66799
DOC. NO.

MONTH

NAME   FIRST   (AY)   (PLEASE PRINT)   LAST   INITIAL

ADDRESS

CITY   STATE

DRIVER
LIC. NO.   STATE

DATE OF   MO.   DAY   YEAR   RACE   SEX   HEIGHT   WEIGHT
BIRTH

EMPLOYERS NAME   TELEPHONE NO.

BUSINESS ADDRESS

NAME OF VEHICLE   DID UNLAWFULLY (PARK) (OPERATE) A
                                          YEAR   BODY TYPE

LICENSE PLATE NO.   REG. DATE
                                          MUNICIPALITY

LOCATION — STREET   REG. DATE

AND DID THEN AND THERE COMMIT THE FOLLOWING OFFENSE(S):

□ SPEEDING   M.P.H. IN _____ M.P.H. ZONE

□ CARELESS DRIVING   (DESCRIBE IN WORDS)   □ RECKLESS DRIVING

DISREGARD OF   IMPROPER OPERATION BY:
□ Traffic signal   □ Stop sign   □ Improper turn   □ Passing on right
□ Officer's signal □ Yield sign   □ Not keeping right □ Passing on curve
                                    □ Passing at curve   □ Crossing center line

OTHER VIOLATION (DESCRIBE IN WORDS)

STATUTE   ORDINANCE NO.   SEC.

PARKING: □ OVERTIME - METER NO. _____
          □ ALL NIGHT   □ DOUBLE
          □ OTHER (DESCRIBE)   □ PROHIBITED AREA

STATUTE   ORDINANCE NO.   SEC.

THE UNDERSIGNED FURTHER STATES THAT HE HAS FAIR AND REASONABLE
GROUNDS TO BELIEVE AND DOES BELIEVE THAT THE PERSON NAMED ABOVE
COMMITTED THE OFFENSE HEREIN SET FORTH, CONTRARY TO LAW.

(DATE)

COURT APPEARANCE REQUIRED □   SIGNATURE OF COMPL.

COURT
APPEARANCE _____ DAY OF _____   IDENTIFICATI.

ADDRESS OF COURT: MON.

"IF YOU

Or, watch

Even John Denver
errs occasionally.

Do not determine to change your life eventually. If you have decided to change your life, it is already changing.

Butterflies don't flutter for lust alone,
except if they're social.

Aloneness, like life, becomes more interesti

hen you realize it's a present.

Nowhere is also Now Here.

Find a piece of it to enjoy.

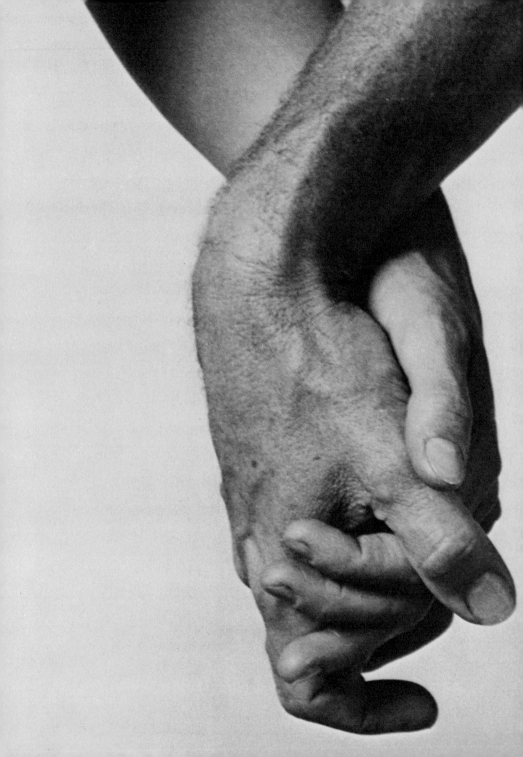

Find a piece of him to enjoy.

If that no longer does it for you,
eat a piece of fresh fruit.
Slowly.

In every pail of garbage there is probably one thing of beauty, crushed. Still, it's more fun going through magazines.

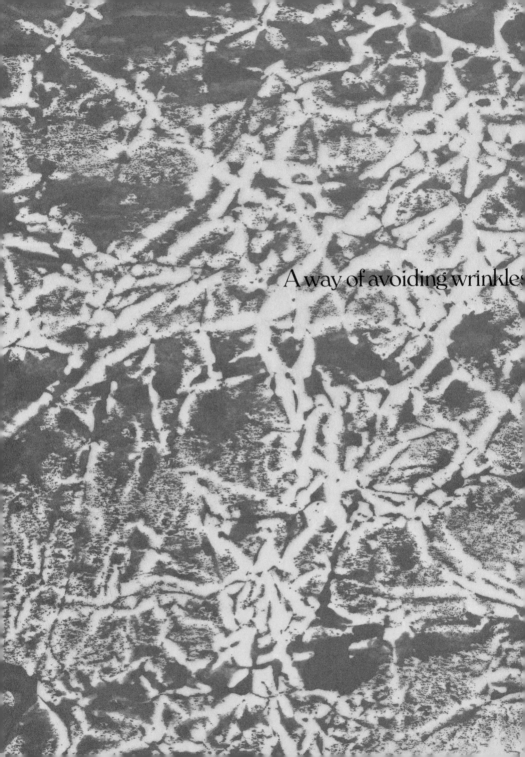

A way of avoiding wrinkles

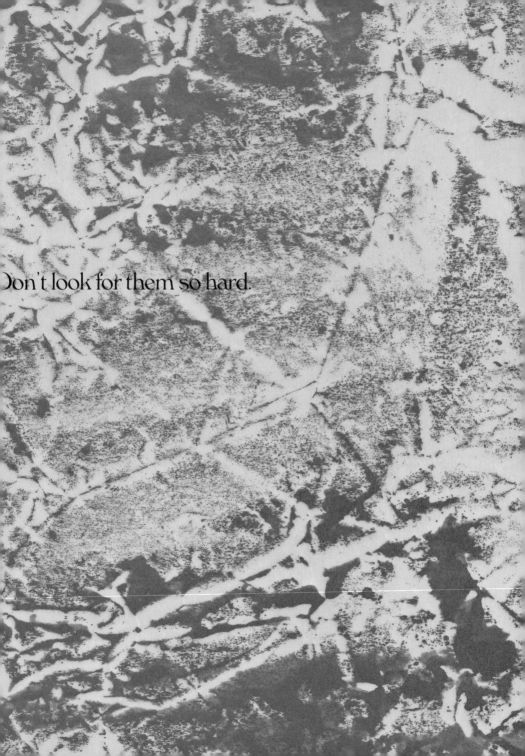

Don't look for them so hard.

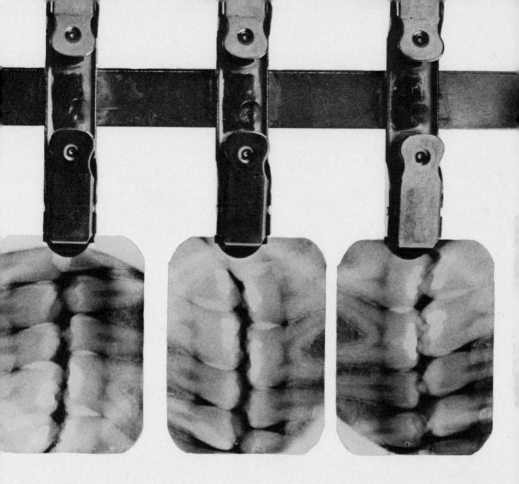

Every human being has a soul, even the dentist.

Prepare witty little ripostes for Gore Vidal,
while folding laundry.

Seem to enjoy Halloween.

See your soul as fabric softener,
built in to keep you from
clinging to things.

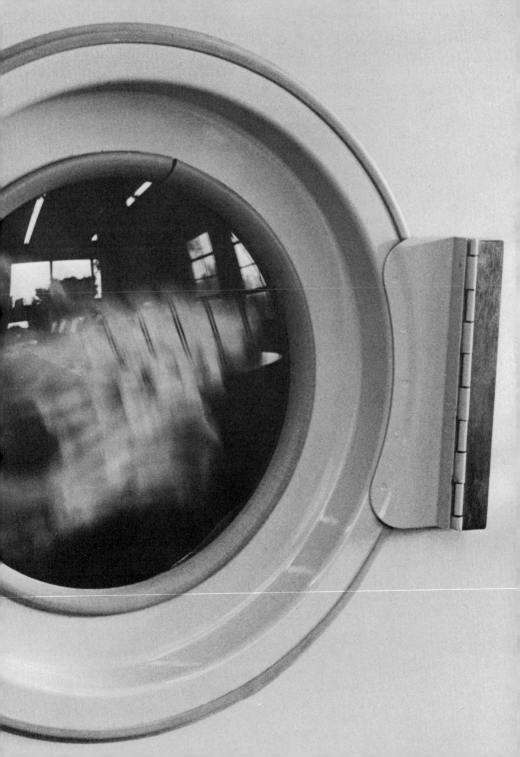

A masochist is Man's best friend.

Get to know your pumpkin.

Think of love as Passion Tempura,
dipped in lightly seasoned flower,
crisped in the hot oil of experience.

Life is a minor debauch.
To keep it really minor is a triumph of character.

Pick out the one picture from all he took last summer that really came out, and praise it.

Do not mention the ones that came out too dark or too light, unless you live in Cleveland.

Stillness, too, is a message.

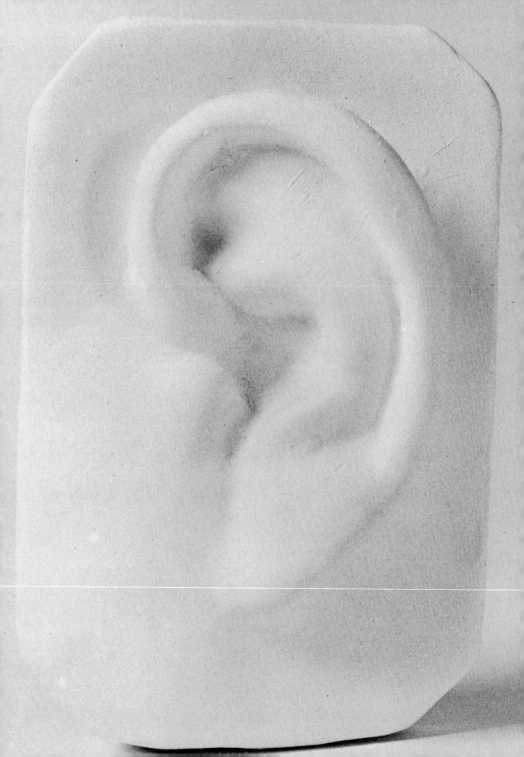

If you live in New York,

get a German shepherd.

Name your plants.
Try to call them after people
they resemble. Do not name
a Wandering Jew Henry.

If you got the boy you loved
in high school, hide this book
between your legs,
where he can't find it.

Do not have lunch with people who tell
Polish jokes, unless they are Polish.

Imagine life as Mrs. Howard Cosell.

Always groom yourself as if you might run
into Warren Beatty, unless you are with
Warren Beatty.

If you are lucky enough to have a maid,
remember if she knew more,
she wouldn't be a maid.

If you are a maid, don't read this, unless it's been left in the bathroom. When you're finished, leave your <u>National Enquirer</u> for her.

Children can be fun, even if they're yours.

Think of your husband as a lover from a previous life, and wonder what you did to deserve him.

Angels are sinners who considered changing.

Translate the words of bores into musical notes, and listen to how pretty they sound.

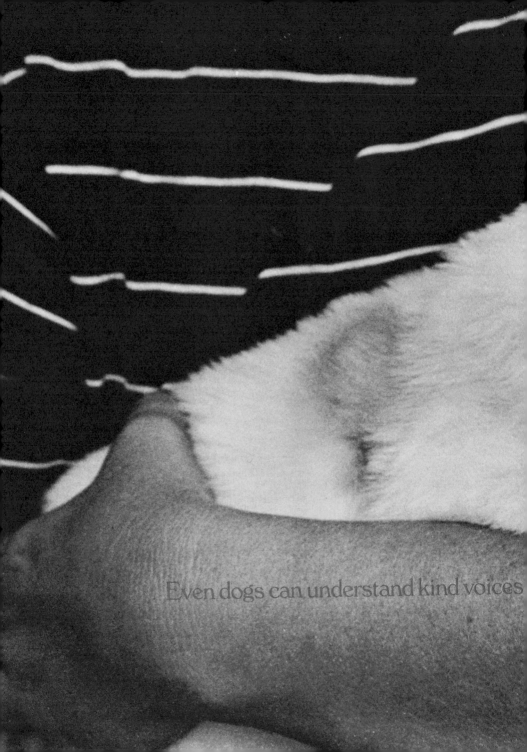

Even dogs can understand kind voices

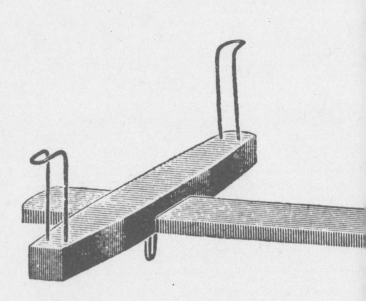

To feel on top of the world, observe it.
At the same time, avoid the news.

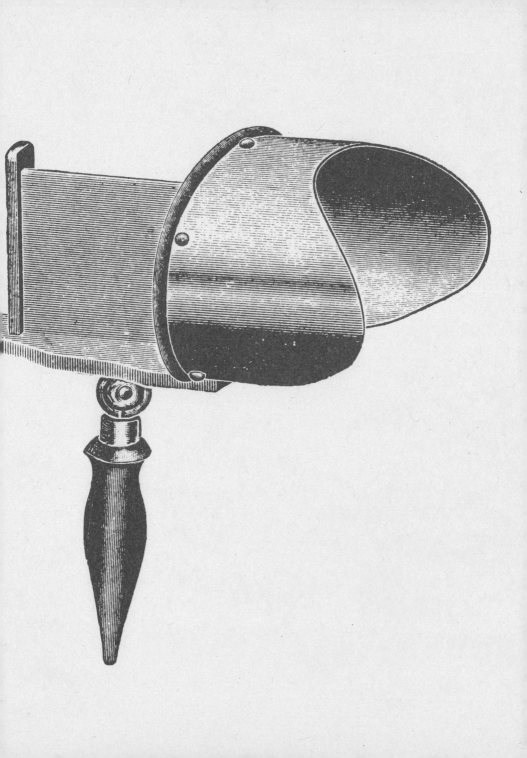

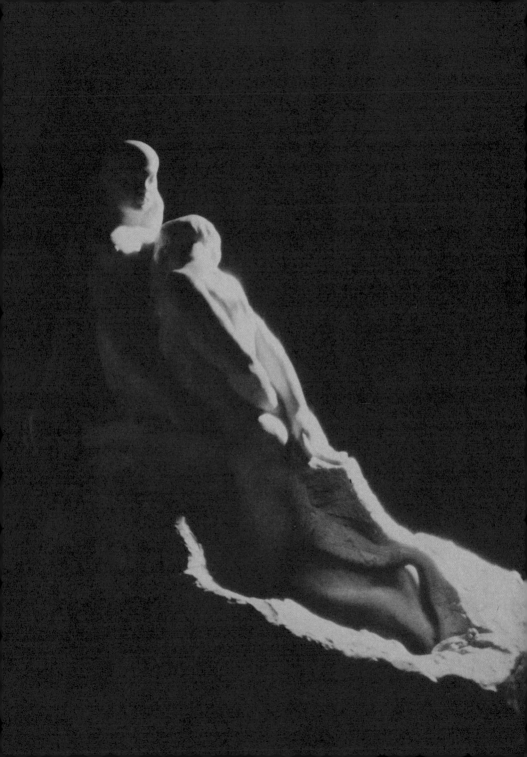

Any man becomes exciting if you think about him hard enough.

A stitch in time saves those
who can do needlepoint.

Too many cooks spoil Burt Reynolds.

To forgive is human, to err divine.

Mark the day that spring begins.
Find a sign of it in nature,
and yourself.

And your husband, if he's up to it.
If not, watch "The Tonight Show."

Find romance in the number nine.
It will follow you everywhere.

Celebrate the day that summer starts by not taking back a present he didn't like for Father's Day.

FIRST
PRIZE

Do not allow the myths that you are uncreative.
Children are a form of art.

Love means never having to date Ryan O'Neal.

Try not to be alarmed that the habit patterns
of your children are being dictated by reruns.

Courage stems from the same word as heart.

Render therefore unto Caesar the thin

which are Elizabeth Taylor's.

If <u>Ms.</u> magazine got mad enough,
it could be Indira Ghandi.

To purify your body, go on a water fast.
Or, hang out with an Aquarius.

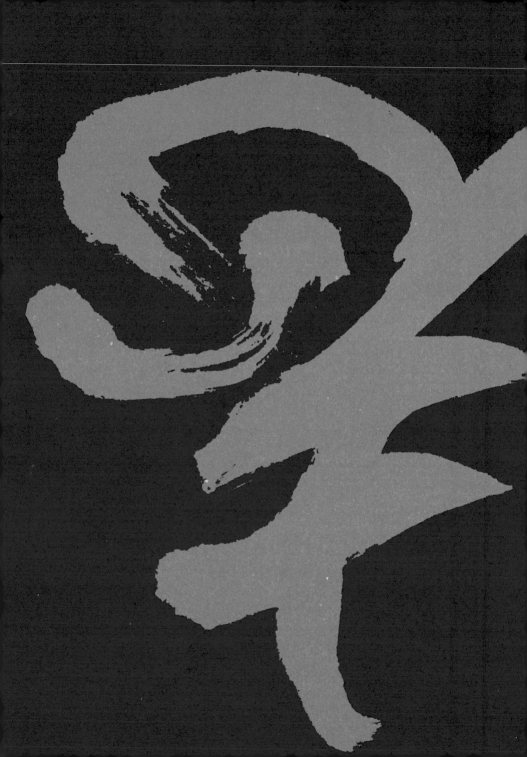

The greatest success is not being driven by success.

What hath Cary Granted?

Imagine life as Cher's manicurist.

Let her who is without cellulite cast the first stone.

If you are Cher's manicurist, put this in the washing machine, where she'll never see it.

What you do to your body,
your body will do back.
Forget that at Baskin-Robbins.

It is hard to find peace at McDonald's.

It is a jesting universe where the longing for first romance couples with acne.

Study a naked tree, its branches threading skyward, and try thinking that design could be accidental.

Then, put the new toilet paper on the roll.

I mean, that's the point. Anybody can get in touch with himself in Tibet.

But if you can get it right, right there in the middle of the marketing, and the million debilitating and humiliating things of which life is sometimes composed,

then so will you be.

In other words:
    If you can keep your head when all
about you are losing theirs, and blaming it
on you, you'll be